Pet Corner / Rincón de las mascotas

SLITHERING SNAKES/ SERPIENTES RESBALADIZAS

By Rose Carraway

Traducción al español: Eduardo Alamán

Gareth Stevens Publishing

Please visit our website, www.garethstevens.com. For a free color catalog of all our high-quality books, call toll free 1-800-542-2595 or fax 1-877-542-2596.

Library of Congress Cataloging-in-Publication Data

Carraway, Rose.
[Slithering snakes. Spanish & English]
Slithering snakes = Serpientes resbaladizas / Rose Carraway.
p. cm. — (Pet corner = Rincón de las mascotas)
Includes index.
ISBN 978-1-4339-6645-3 (library binding)
1. Snakes as pets—Juvenile literature. I. Title. II. Title: Serpientes resbaladizas.
SF459.S5C3618 2012
639.3'96—dc23
2011024842

First Edition

Published in 2012 by
Gareth Stevens Publishing
111 East 14th Street, Suite 349
New York, NY 10003

Editor: Katie Kawa
Designer: Andrea Davison-Bartolotta
Spanish Translation: Eduardo Alamán

Photo credits: Cover, pp. 1, 7, 9, 11, 13, 15, 19, 21, 24 (bowl, tongue) Shutterstock.com; p. 5 Michael Blann/Stone/Getty Images; p. 17 davespilbrow/Flickr/Getty Images; p. 23 Jupiterimages/Brand X Pictures/Thinkstock; p. 24 (cage) iStockphoto.com.

Printed in the United States of America

CPSIA compliance information: Batch #CW12GS: For further information contact Gareth Stevens, New York, New York at 1-800-542-2595.

Contents

Contenido

Pet snakes come
in many sizes.
They can be
many colors, too.

Las serpientes mascota
pueden tener muchos
tamaños. También
tienen muchos colores.

Snakes have no legs!

¡Las serpientes no tienen patas!

A pet snake lives
in a glass cage.

Las serpientes mascota
viven en tanques de
vidrio.

A snake likes
to feel safe.
It hides in its cage.

A las serpientes les
gusta sentirse seguras.
Se esconden en su
tanque.

A pet snake needs
a water bowl.

Las serpientes mascota
necesitan un recipiente
con agua.

It drinks the water.
It lies in the water, too.

Las serpientes beben el agua. También se recuestan en ella.

Snakes eat other animals. They eat mice and rats.

Las serpientes comen otros animales. Comen ratones y ratas.

A snake uses
its tongue to smell.
It works like a nose.

Las serpientes usan
su lengua para oler.
La lengua funciona
como una nariz.

Words to Know/ Palabras que debes saber

bowl/
(el) recipiente

cage/
(el) tanque

tongue/
(la) lengua

Index / Índice

TRICKS WITH BIKES
TRUCOS CON LA MOTO

Connor Dayton

Traducción al español:
Eduardo Alamán

PowerKiDS press & Editorial Buenas Letras™

New York

Published in 2007 by The Rosen Publishing Group, Inc.
29 East 21st Street, New York, NY 10010

First Edition

Editor: Jennifer Way
Book Design: Erica Clendening
Layout Design: Kate Laczynski and Lissette González
Photo Researcher: Sam Cha

Photo Credits: Cover, pp. 1, 11, 13, 17, 23 image copyright Taolmor, 2006. Used under license from Shutterstock, Inc.; p. 5 image copyright Brad Angus, 2006. Used under license from Shutterstock, Inc.; p. 7 image copyright Diane Gonzales, 2006. Used under license from Shutterstock, Inc.; p. 9 image copyright Asian, 2006. Used under license from Shutterstock, Inc.; pp. ; p. 15 © Dan Regan/Getty Images; pp. 19, 21 © Robert Cianflone/Getty Images.

Cataloging Data

Dayton, Connor.
Tricks with bikes / Connor Dayton; traducción al español: Eduardo Alamán. — 1st ed.
p. cm. — (Motorcycles: Made for Speed—Motocicletas a toda velocidad)
Includes index.
ISBN-13: 978-1-4042-7615-4 (library binding)
ISBN-10: 1-4042-7615-7 (library binding)
1. Stunt cycling—Juvenile literature. 2. Spanish language materials. I. Title.

Manufactured in the United States of America

CONTENTS

CONTENIDO

There are many kinds of motorcycle tricks. Riding on one wheel is called a wheelie.

Se pueden hacer muchos trucos con las motocicletas. En este truco llamado "caballito", el piloto maneja sobre la rueda de atrás.

SUZUKI
GSX R
SUZUKI

Spinning a wheel against a **paved** road is called a burnout. It makes a lot of smoke and noise.

Hacer rodar una rueda contra el **pavimento** es un truco que causa mucho humo y ruido. Se llama *burnout*, porque "*burn*" quiere decir quemar.

Arai
Tires

Lots of tricks are done up in the air. These kinds of tricks start with a jump.

Muchos trucos se hacen en el aire. Estos trucos comienzan con un salto.

117

When a trick is done high in the air, the rider can push off of the motorcycle.

Cuando el truco es muy alto en el aire, el piloto puede salirse de la moto.

People can hold
pet snakes.
They have to be
very careful!

Las personas pueden
agarrar a las serpientes
mascota. ¡Hay que
hacerlo con cuidado!

YAMAHA
YAMAHA

A rider might try to stand on the bike as part of a trick. Bike tricks might be **dangerous**, but they are fun to watch.

Algunos pilotos tratan de pararse en sus motos. Estos trucos pueden ser **peligrosos**, pero resultan divertidos para los espectadores.

This rider is standing on the handlebars of the bike. This is a hard trick to do.

Este piloto está parado en el manubrio de su moto. Este es un truco muy difícil.

For some **stunts** the rider will let go of the bike. It looks like this rider is flying over his bike!

En algunas **maniobras**, el piloto se separa de la motocicleta. ¡Parece que el piloto vuela sobre su moto!

CHUCK
ARO
FOX

Stunt riders who are really good can even do **flips** on their bikes!

¡Los mejores pilotos de maniobras pueden hacer **volteretas** con sus motos!

People do tricks on all different kinds of bikes. This person is doing a jump on a minibike.

Se pueden hacer trucos en cualquier clase de motocicleta. Este piloto brinca en una mini-moto.

SCOTT
22
DUNLOP
POWERHOUSE

There are games called Stunt Wars, in which riders do tricks for groups of people.

En las competiciones llamadas *Stunt Wars,* o Guerras de maniobras, los pilotos muestran sus trucos a otras personas.

HONDA
globe
POWERHOUSE

Glossary / Glosario

dangerous (DAYN-jeh-rus) Might make something hurt.

flips (FLIPS) Turns from head to toe in the air.

paved (PAYVD) Covered with something hard and human made.

stunts (STUNTS) Acts that are hard to do.

---

maniobras (las) Movimientos que son difíciles de hacer.

pavimento (el) Cubierta dura fabricada por los seres humanos.

peligroso(a) Que puede causar daño.

volteretas (las) Vueltas que se dan en el aire.

Index

Índice